From Morn to Midnight

A play in seven scenes

Georg Kaiser,
Ashley Dukes

Alpha Editions

This edition published in 2020

ISBN : 9789354007026

Design and Setting By
Alpha Editions
email - alphaedis@gmail.com

As per information held with us this book is in Public Domain. This book is a reproduction of an important historical work. Alpha Editions uses the best technology to reproduce historical work in the same manner it was first published to preserve its original nature. Any marks or number seen are left intentionally to preserve its true form.

From Morn to Midnight
A PLAY IN SEVEN SCENES

BY GEORG KAISER

TRANSLATED FROM THE GERMAN BY
ASHLEY DUKES
(The Theatre Guild version)

WITH EIGHT ILLUSTRATIONS FROM PHOTOGRAPHS OF THE
THEATRE GUILD PRODUCTION

NEW YORK
BRENTANO'S
Publishers

The cast of the THEATRE GUILD PRODUCTION as originally presented at the GARRICK THEATRE, May 21st, 1922.

FROM MORN TO MIDNIGHT

A Play in seven scenes by GEORG KAISER
Translation by ASHLEY DUKES
Staged by Frank Reicher
Settings designed by Lee Simonson

The cast of characters in the order of their appearance

Cashier	Frank Reicher
Stout Gentleman	Ernest Cossart
Clerk	Sears Taylor
Messenger Boy	Francis Sadtler
Lady	Helen Westley
Bank Manager	Henry Travers
Muffled Gentleman	Allyn Joslyn
Serving Maid	Adele St. Maur
Porter	Charles Cheltenham
The Lady's Son	Edgar Stehli
The Cashier's Mother	Kathryn Wilson
His Daughters	{ Lelia May Aultman { Julia Cobb
His Wife	Ernita Lascelles
First Gentleman	Walton Butterfield
Second Gentleman	Philip Leigh
Third Gentleman	Herman Goodman
Fourth Gentleman	Samuel Baron
Fifth Gentleman	William Crowell
Salvation Lass	Helen Sheridan
Waiter	Edgar Stehli
First Mask	Clelia Benjamin
Second Mask	Adele St. Maur
Third Mask	Caroline Hancock
Fourth Mask	Annette Ponse
First Guest	Sears Taylor
Second Guest	Allyn Joslyn
Third Guest	Sam Rosen
Officer of Salvation Army	Ernita Lascelles
First Soldier of Salvation Army	Philip Leigh
First Penitent	Philip Loeb
Second Soldier of Salvation Army	Camille Pastorfield
Second Penitent	Helen Westley

Third Soldier of Salvation Army . . .	Henry Travers
Third Penitent	Ernest Cossart
Fourth Soldier of Salvation Army . . .	William Crowell
Policeman	Stanley Howlett

CROWD AT VELODROME AND SALVATION ARMY HALL:

Mary Beechwood, Peggy Vaughan, Albert Powers, Annette Ponse, Teddy Tolputt, Estelle Corcos, Barbara Kitson, Lester Nass, Kenneth Campbell, Genevieve Corbin, Sarah Fishman, Margaret Wernimont, Philip Loeb.

SCENE I—The Interior of a Provincial Bank
SCENE II—The Writing Room of a Hotel
SCENE III—A Field in Deep Snow
SCENE IV—The Parlor in the Cashier's Home

INTERMISSION

SCENE V—The Steward's Box at a Velodrome during Bicycle Races
SCENE VI—A Private Supper Room in a Cabaret
SCENE VII—A Salvation Army Hall

In a Small Town and a City in Germany at the Present Time

Stage Manager Jacob Weiser

Assistant Stage Managers { Sears Taylor
Allyn Joslyn

Stage, screen and amateur rights for this translation and the original play are owned and controlled by The Theatre Guild, Inc., 65 west 35th St., New York City. No performances or public readings may be given without their written consent.

INTRODUCTION

Georg Kaiser, a German dramatist, has published some fifteen plays since 1911, twelve of which appeared during the war. Of these "Von Morgens bis Mitternachts" (1916), lately performed in Berlin under the direction of Max Reinhardt, is here translated.

The author has been called an "expressionist," and is by way of being considered as the founder of a new dramatic school; doubtless because the need is felt to describe succinctly an art which consists in a series of graphic gestures, like a vigorous clenching of the smooth palm of actuality. It is true that Georg Kaiser brings a new method into the theatre. His singular economy of words is as it were the obverse of his lively but disciplined invention; and while these qualities have made the task of translation no simpler, they will do something to establish the international or non-national character of the work. To the most unfriendly gaze Georg Kaiser will appear to be a link between the three-dimensional stage and the screen, and a portent therefore not to be despised. But others who look deeper will read in

INTRODUCTION

the movement of his nameless hurrying throng of characters the poet's reflection of a universal gesture, and in their faces his image of a common unrest.

ASHLEY DUKES

CHARACTERS

Bank Cashier
Mother
Wife
First and Second Daughters
Bank Manager
Clerk
Porter
Stout Gentleman
Muffled Gentleman
Messenger Boy
Serving Maid
Lady
Son
Waiter (*In Hotel*)
Five Jewish Gentleman
Four Female Masks
Waiter (*In Cabaret*)
Gentleman in Evening Dress
Salvation Lass
Officer and Soldiers (*Of Salvation Army*)
Penitents
Crowd (*At Salvation Meeting*)
Policeman

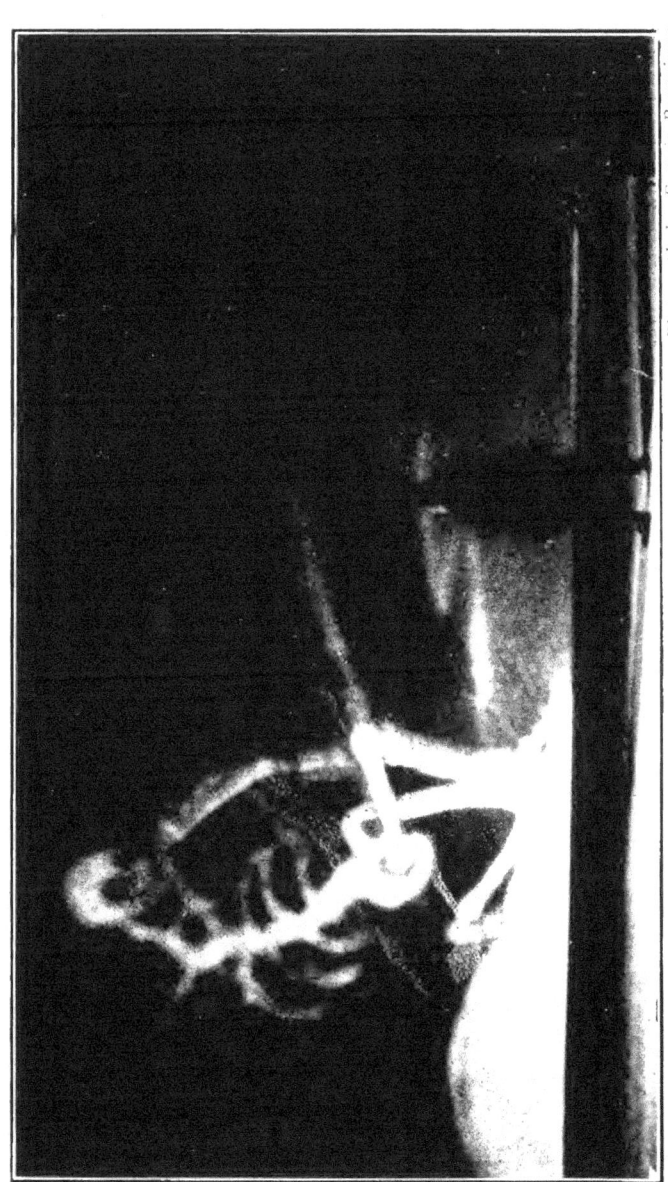

Setting by Lee Simonson Photograph by Francis Bruguière

SCENE III. FROM THE THEATRE GUILD PRODUCTION

SYNOPSIS OF SCENES

I
INTERIOR OF A SMALL BANK.

II
WRITING-ROOM OF A HOTEL.

III
FIELD DEEP IN SNOW.

IV
PARLOUR IN CASHIER'S HOUSE.

V
STEWARD'S BOX AT A VELODROME, DURING CYCLE RACES.

VI
PRIVATE SUPPER-ROOM IN A CABARET.

VII
SALVATION ARMY HALL.

In a small Town and a City in Germany at the present time.

FROM MORN TO MIDNIGHT

Setting by Lee Simonson   Photograph by Francis Bruguière

SCENE 1. FROM THE THEATRE GUILD PRODUCTION

From Morn To Midnight

SCENE I

SCENE: *Interior of a provincial Bank.*
On the right, pigeon-holes and a door inscribed MANAGER. *Another door in the middle:* STRONG ROOM. *Entrance from the lower left. In front of the* CASHIER'S *cage on the left hand side is a cane sofa, and in front of it a small table with a water-bottle and glass.*

RISE: *The* CASHIER *at the counter and the* CLERK *at a desk, both writing. On the cane sofa sits a* STOUT GENTLEMAN, *wheezing. In front of the counter stands a* MESSENGER BOY, *staring at the door, through which some one has just gone out.*

CASHIER

[*Raps on the counter.*]
[MESSENGER BOY *turns, hands in a cheque.*]
[CASHIER *examines it, writes, takes a handful of silver from a drawer, counts it, pushes a small pile across the counter.*]
[MESSENGER BOY *sweeps the money into a linen bag.*]

Stout Gentleman

[*Rising*]: Now the fat fellows take their turn. [*He pulls out a bag. Enter* Lady, *expensive furs; rustle of silk.* Stout Gentleman *stops short.*]

Lady

[*Smiles involuntarily in his direction.*] At last!
[Stout Gentleman *makes a wry face.*]
[Cashier *taps the counter impatiently.*]
[Lady *looks at* Stout Gentleman.]

Stout Gentleman

[*Giving place to her*]: The fat fellows can wait.
[Lady *bows distantly, comes to counter.*]
[Cashier *taps as before.*]

Lady

[*Opens her handbag, takes out a letter and hands it to* Cashier]: A letter of credit. Three thousand, please. [Cashier *takes the envelope, turns it over, hands it back.*] I beg your pardon. [*She pulls out the folded letter and offers it again.*]
[Cashier *turns it over, hands it back.*]

Lady

[*Unfolds the letter. Hands it to him.*]

Three thousand, please.
[CASHIER *glances at it, puts it in front of the* CLERK. CLERK *takes the letter, rises, goes out by the door inscribed* MANAGER.]

STOUT GENTLEMAN

[*Retiring to sofa*]: I can wait. The fat fellows can always wait.

[CASHIER *begins counting silver.*]

LADY

In notes, if you don't mind.
[CASHIER *ignores her.*]

MANAGER

[*Youthful, plump, comes in with the letter in his hand*]: Who is—
[*He stops short on seeing the lady.*]
[CLERK *resumes work at his desk.*]

STOUT GENTLEMAN

Ahem! Good morning.

MANAGER

[*Glancing at him*]: How goes it?

STOUT GENTLEMAN

[*Tapping his belly*]: Oh, rounding out—rounding out!

MANAGER

[*Laughs shortly. Turning to Lady*]: I understand you want to draw on us?

LADY

Three thousand marks.

MANAGER

I would pay you three—[*glancing at letter*]—three thousand with pleasure, but—

LADY

Is anything wrong with the letter?

MANAGER

[*Suave, important*]: It's in the proper form.
[*Reading the headlines*]: "Not exceeding twelve thousand"—quite correct. [*Spelling out the address.*] "B-A-N-K-O"—

LADY

My bank in Florence assured me—

MANAGER

Your bank in Florence is quite all right.

LADY

Then I don't see why—

MANAGER

I suppose you applied for this letter?

LADY

Of course.

MANAGER

Twelve thousand—payable at such cities—

LADY

As I should touch on my trip.

MANAGER

And you must have given your bank in Florence duplicate signatures.

LADY

Certainly. To be sent to the banks mentioned in the list to identify me.

MANAGER

[*Consults letter*]: Ah!
[*Looks up*]: We have received no letter of advice.

STOUT GENTLEMAN

[*Coughs; winks at the* MANAGER.]

LADY

That means I must wait until. . . .

MANAGER

Well, we must have something to go upon!
[MUFFLED GENTLEMAN, *in fur cap and shawl, comes in and takes his place at the counter. He darts angry glances at the* LADY.]

LADY

I was quite unprepared for this. . . .

MANAGER

[*With a clumsy laugh*]: As you see, Madame, we are even less prepared; in fact—not at all.

LADY

I need the money so badly. . . .
[STOUT GENTLEMAN *laughs aloud.*]

MANAGER

Who doesn't?
[STOUT GENTLEMAN *neighs with delight.*]
[*Looking round for an audience.*]
Myself, for instance—
[*To the impatient* MUFFLED CUSTOMER.]
You have more time than I—don't you see I'm busy with this LADY? Now, Madame, what do you expect me to do—pay you money on your—ah—
[STOUT GENTLEMAN *titters.*]

LADY

[*Quickly*]: I'm staying at the Elephant.

MANAGER

[STOUT GENTLEMAN *wheezes with laughter.*]
I am very glad to know your address.

I always lunch there.

LADY

Can't the proprietor vouch for me?

MANAGER

Has he already had the pleasure?
[STOUT GENTLEMAN *rocks with delight.*]

LADY

Well, I have my luggage with me . . .

MANAGER

Am I to examine it?

LADY

A most embarrassing position. I can't. . . .

MANAGER

Then we're in the same boat. You can't—I can't—that's the situation.
[*He returns the letter.*]

LADY

What do you advise me to do?

MANAGER

This is a snug little town of ours—it has surroundings— The Elephant is a well-known house . . . you'll make pleasant acquaintances of one sort or another . . . and time will pass—days—nights—well you know?

LADY

I don't in the least mind passing a few days here.

MANAGER

Your fellow-guests will be delighted to contribute something for your entertainment.

LADY

But I must have three thousand to-day!

MANAGER

[*To* STOUT GENTLEMAN]: Will anybody here underwrite a lady from abroad for three thousand marks?

LADY

I couldn't think of accepting that. I shall be in my room at the hotel. When the letter of advice arrives, will you please notify me at once by telephone?

MANAGER

Personally, Madame, if you wish.

LADY

In whatever way is quickest. [*She folds up the letter, replaces it in the envelope, and puts both into her handbag.*] I shall call again in any case this afternoon.

MANAGER

At your service. [LADY *bows coldly, goes out.* MUFFLED GENTLEMAN *moves up to counter, on which he leans, crackling his cheque impatiently.* MANAGER *ignoring him, looks merrily at the* STOUT GENTLEMAN. STOUT GENTLEMAN *sniffs the air. Laughs.*] All the fragrance of Italy, eh? Straight from the perfume bottle. [STOUT GENTLEMAN *fans himself with his hand.*] Warm, eh?

STOUT GENTLEMAN

[*Pours out water*]: Three thousand is not bad. [*Drinks.*] I guess three hundred wouldn't sound bad to her either.

MANAGER

Perhaps you would like to make a lower offer at the Elephant?—in her room?

STOUT GENTLEMAN

No use for fat fellows.

MANAGER

Our bellies protect our morals. [MUFFFLED GENTLEMAN *raps impatiently on the counter. Indifferently.*] Well?
[*He takes the cheque, smoothes it out, and hands it to the* CASHIER.]
[MESSENGER BOY *stares after the departing* LADY, *then at the last speakers, finally stumbles over the* STOUT GENTLEMAN *on the sofa.*]

STOUT GENTLEMAN

[*Robbing him of his wallet*]: There, my boy, that's what comes of making eyes at pretty ladies. [Now you've lost your money. [MESSENGER BOY *looks shyly at him.*] How are you going to explain to your boss? [MESSENGER BOY *laughs.*] Remember this for the rest of your life! [*Returning the wallet.*] Your eyes run away and you bolt after them. You wouldn't be the first. [MESSENGER BOY *goes out.*]

[CASHIER *has counted out some small silver.*]

MANAGER

And they trust money to a young fool like that.

STOUT GENTLEMAN

Stupid!

MANAGER

People should be more careful. That boy will abscond the first chance he gets—a born embezzler. [*To* MUFFLED GENTLEMAN]: Is anything wrong? [MUFFLED GENTLEMAN *examines every coin.*] That's a twenty-five pfennig piece. Forty-five pfennigs altogether; that's all that's coming to you. [MUFFLED GENTLEMAN *pockets his money with great ceremony; buttons his coat over the pocket.*]

STOUT GENTLEMAN

[*Ironically*]: You ought to deposit your capital in the vault.

[*Rising*]: Now it's time for the fat fellows to unload.
[MUFFLED GENTLEMAN *turns away from counter, and goes out.*]

MANAGER

[*To* STOUT GENTLEMAN, *breezily*]: What are you bringing us this morning?

STOUT GENTLEMAN

[*Sets his attaché case on the counter and takes out a pocket-book*]: With all the confidence that your elegant clientele inspires. [*He offers his hand.*]

MANAGER

[*Taking it*]: In any case we are immune to a pretty face when it comes to business.

STOUT GENTLEMAN

[*Counting out his money*]: How old was she, at a guess?

MANAGER

I haven't seen her without rouge—yet.

STOUT GENTLEMAN

What's she doing here?

MANAGER

We'll hear that to-night at the Elephant.

STOUT GENTLEMAN

But who's she after?

MANAGER

All of us, perhaps, before she gets through.

STOUT GENTLEMAN

What can she do with three thousand in this town?

MANAGER

Evidently she needs them.

STOUT GENTLEMAN

I wish her luck.

MANAGER

With what!

STOUT GENTLEMAN

Getting her three thousand if she can.

MANAGER

From me?

STOUT GENTLEMAN

It doesn't matter from whom! [*They laugh.*]

MANAGER

I'm curious to see when that letter of advice from Florence will arrive.

STOUT GENTLEMAN

If it arrives!

MANAGER

Ah! If it arrives!

STOUT GENTLEMAN

We might make a collection for her benefit.

MANAGER

I dare say that's what she has in mind.

Stout Gentleman

You don't need to tell me.

Manager

Did you draw a winning number in the last lottery? [*They laugh.*]

Stout Gentleman

[*To* Cashier]: Take this. What's the difference if our money draws interest here or outside. Here—open an account for the Realty Construction Co.

Manager

[*Sharply, to* Clerk]: Account: "Realty Construction Co."

Stout Gentleman

There's more to come.

Manager

The more the merrier. We can use it just now.

STOUT GENTLEMAN

Sixty thousand marks, fifty thousand in paper, ten thousand in gold.
[CASHIER *begins counting.*]

MANAGER

[*After a pause*]: And how are you, otherwise?

STOUT GENTLEMAN

[*To* CASHIER, *who pauses to examine a note*]: Yes, that one's patched.

MANAGER

We'll accept it, of course. We shall soon be rid of it. I'll reserve it for our fair client from Florence. She wore patches too.

STOUT GENTLEMAN

But behind these you find—a thousand marks.

MANAGER

Face value.

STOUT GENTLEMAN

[*Laughing immoderately*]: Face value—that's good!

MANAGER

The face value! Here's your receipt. [*Choking with laughter.*] Sixty—thousand—

STOUT GENTLEMAN

[*Takes it, reads*]: Sixty—thou—

MANAGER

Face.

STOUT GENTLEMAN

Value. [*They shake hands.*]

MANAGER

[*In tears*]: I'll see you to-night.

STOUT GENTLEMAN

[*Nods*]: The face—the face—value! [*He buttons his overcoat, and goes out laughing.*]

[MANAGER *wipes the tears from his pince-nez;* CASHIER *fastens the notes together in bundles.*]

MANAGER

This lady from Florence—who claims to come from Florence—has a vision like that ever visited you in your cage before? Furs—perfume! The fragrance lingers—you breathe adventure. Superbly staged. Italy . . . Enchantment—fairytale — Riviera — Mentone — Pordighera — Nice —Monte Carlo,—where oranges blossom, fraud blooms, too. Swindlers—down there every squarefoot of earth breeds them. They organize crusades. The gang disperses to the four winds—preferably small towns—off the beaten track. Then—apparitions—billowing silks—furs—women—modern sirens. Refrains from the sunny south—o bella Napoli! One glance and you're stripped to your undershirt—to the bare skin—to the naked, naked skin. [*He drums with a pencil on the* CASHIER'S *hand.*] Depend upon it, this bank in Florence knows as much about the lady as the man in the moon. The whole affair is a swindle, carefully arranged. And the web was woven not in Florence, but in Monte Carlo. That's the place to keep in mind. Take my word for it, you've just seen one of the gadflies that thrive in the swamp of the Casino. We shall never see her again. The first attempt missed fire; she'll scarcely risk a second! I joke about it but I have a keen eye—when you're a banker—I really should have tipped off the police! Well, it doesn't concern me—besides, banks must be discreet. Keep your eye on the out-of-town papers,—the police news. When you find something there about an adventuress, safe under lock and key—then we'll talk about it again. You'll see I was right—then we'll hear more of our Florentine lady than we'll ever see of her and her furs again. [*Exit.*]

[CASHIER *seals up rolls of bank notes.*]

PORTER

[*Enters with letters, hands them to* CLERK]: One registered letter. I want the receipt.

[CLERK *stamps receipt form, hands it to* PORTER. PORTER *re-arranges glass and water-bottle on the table, and goes out.* CLERK *takes the letters into* MANAGER's *room, and returns.*]

LADY

[*Re-enters; comes quickly to the counter*]: I beg your pardon.

CASHIER

[*Stretches out his hand, without looking at her. Raps.*]

Lady

[*Louder*]: If you please! [CASHIER *raps on the counter.*] I don't want to trouble the Manager a second time. [CASHIER *raps on the counter.*] Please tell me—would it be possible for me to leave you the letter of credit for the whole sum, and to receive an advance of three thousand in part payment? [CASHIER *raps impatiently.*] I should be willing to deposit my diamonds as security, if required. Any jeweler in the town will appraise them for you. [*She takes off a glove and pulls at her bracelet.* SERVING MAID *comes in quickly, plumps down on sofa, and begins rummaging in her marketbasket.* LADY *startled by the commotion, looks round. As she leans on the counter her hand sinks into the* CASHIER'S. CASHIER *bends over the hand which lies in his own. His spectacles glitter, his glance travels slowly upward from her wrist.* SERVING MAID *with a sigh of relief, discovers the cheque she is looking for.* LADY *nods kindly in her direction.* SERVING MAID *replaces vegetables, etc., in her basket.* LADY *turning again to the counter, meets the eyes of the* CASHIER. CASHIER *smiles at her.*]

Lady

[*Drawing back her hand*]: Of course I shall not ask the bank to do anything irregular. [*She puts the bracelet on her wrist; the clasp refuses to catch. Stretching out her arm to the* CASHIER]: Would you be so kind? I'm clumsy with the left hand. [CASHIER *stares at her as if mesmerized. His spectacles, bright points of light, seem almost to be swallowed up in the cavity of his wide-open eyes. To* SERVING MAID]: You can help me, mademoiselle. [SERVING MAID *does so.*] Now the safety catch. [*With a little cry*]: You're pinching my flesh. Ah, that's better. Thank you so much. [*She bows to the* CASHIER *and goes out.* SERVING MAID *coming to the counter, planks down her cheque.* CASHIER *takes it in trembling hands, the slip of paper flutters and crackles; he fumbles under the counter, then counts out money.*]

SERVING MAID

[*Looking at the pile of coins*]: That isn't all mine. [CASHIER *writes.* CLERK *becomes observant.*]

SERVING MAID

[*To* CLERK]: But it's too much! [CLERK *looks at* CASHIER. CASHIER *rakes in part of the money.*] Still too much! [CASHIER *ignores her and continues writing.* SERVING MAID *shaking her head, puts the money in her basket and goes out.*]

Cashier

[*Hoarsely*]: Get me a glass of water! [Clerk *hurries from behind the counter; comes to table.*] That's been standing. Fresh water—cold water—from the faucet. [Clerk *hurries out with glass.* Cashier *goes quickly to electric bell, and rings.* Porter *enters from the hall.*] Get me fresh water.

Porter

I'm not allowed to go so far from the door.

Cashier

[*Hoarsely*]: For me. Not that slime. I want water from the faucet. [Porter *seizes water-bottle and hurries out.* Cashier *quickly crams his pockets with bank notes. Then he takes his coat from a peg, throws it over his arm, and puts on his hat. He lifts a flap in the counter, passes through, and goes out.*]

Manager

[*Absorbed in reading a letter, enters from his room*]: Here's the letter of advice from Florence, after all! [Clerk *enters with a glass of water.* Porter *enters with a full water-bottle.*]

MANAGER

[*Looking up*]: What the devil. . . ?

CURTAIN

Setting by Lee Simonson Photograph by Francis Bruguière
SCENE II. FROM THE THEATRE GUILD PRODUCTION

SCENE II.

SCENE: *Writing-room of a hotel. Glass door in back ground. On right, desk with telephone. On the left, sofa and arm chair with table and newspapers.*

LADY

[*Writes.* SON, *in hat and coat, enters, carrying under his arm a large flat object wrapped in green baize. With surprise*]: Have you brought it with you?

SON

Hush! The wine dealer is downstairs. The old fool is afraid I'll run away with it.

LADY

But I thought this morning he was glad to get rid of it.

SON

Now he's suspicious.

LADY

You must have given yourself away.

SON

I did let him see I was pleased.

LADY

[*Smiling*]: That would open a blind man's eyes.

SON

Let it. But don't be afraid, Mother, the price is the same as it was this morning.

LADY

Is the man waiting for his money?

SON

Let him wait.

LADY

But, my dear boy, I must tell you—

SON

[*Kissing her*]: Hush, Mother. This is a great

moment. You mustn't look until I say so. [*He takes off his hat and cloak, puts the picture on a chair and lifts the green baize covering.*]

LADY

Ready?

SON

[*In a low tone*]: Mother! [LADY *turns in her chair. Comes to her, puts his arm round her neck.*] Well?

LADY

That was never meant to hang in a restaurant.

SON

It was turned to the wall. The old fellow had pasted his own photograph on the back of it.

LADY

Was that included in the price?

SON

[*Laughs*]: Tell me, what do you think of it?

LADY

I find it—very naïve.

SON

Marvelous, isn't it? Extraordinary considering it's a Cranach.

LADY

Do you really prize it as a picture?

SON

Of course! But just look at the peculiar conception—unique for Cranach. And a new treatment of this subject in the entire history of art. Where can you find anything like it—in the Pitti—the Uffizi—the Vatican? Even the Louvre has nothing to compare with it. Here we have without doubt the first and only erotic conception of Adam and Eve. The apple is still in the grass—the serpent leers from behind the indescribable green foliage—and that means that the drama is played in Paradise itself and not in the banishment. That's the original sin—the real fall! Cranach painted dozens of Adams and Eves—standing stiffly—always separated—with the apple bough between them. In those pictures Cranach says simply: they knew each other.

But in this picture for the first time, he cries exultantly they loved each other. Here a German proves himself a master of an eroticism intensely southern in its feeling. [*In front of the picture.*] And yet what restraint in this ecstasy! This line of the man's arm as it slants across the woman's hip. The horizontal line of her thighs and the opposing line of his—never weary the eyes. These flesh tones make their love a living thing—doesn't it affect you that way?

LADY

I find it as naïve as your picture.

SON

What does that mean?

LADY

Please hide it in your room.

SON

I won't get its full effect until we get home. This Cranach in Florence. Of course, I'll have to postpone finishing my book. I must digest this first. A man must live with a thing like this before he dares write about it. Just now I am overwhelmed. Think of finding this picture here—on the first stage of our trip!

Lady

But you were almost certain that it must be in this neighborhood.

Son

I am dazed nevertheless. Isn't it amazing! I am lucky.

Lady

This is simply the result of your own careful research.

Son

But not without your generosity? Your help?

Lady

It makes me as happy as it does you.

Son

Your patience is endless. I tear you from your beautiful quiet life in Fiesole. You are an Italian, but I drag you through Germany in mid-winter. You live in sleeping cars or third-rate hotels; rub elbows with Tom, Dick, Harry!

Lady

[*Smiling—patting his cheek*]: Yes, I have had my fill of that.

Son

·But now I promise you to hurry. I'm madly impatient to get this treasure safely home. Let's take the three o'clock train. Will you give me the three thousand marks?

Lady

I haven't them.

Son

But the owner is here, in the hotel.

Lady

The bank couldn't pay me. The letter of advice has somehow been delayed.

SON

I've promised him the money.

LADY

Then you must return the picture until the letter arrives.

SON

Can't we hurry it in any way?

LADY

[*Smiles*]: I've written a telegram; I'll have it sent now. You see, we traveled so quickly that —[WAITER *knocks at the door. Phone rings.*] Yes?

WAITER

Some one from the bank.

LADY

Send him up. [*To* SON.] They must be sending the money.

Son

Call me as soon as you've got it. I'd rather keep an eye on the old man.

Lady

I'll send for you.

Son

Then I'll wait downstairs. [*Pauses in front of picture.* Lady *closes her portfolio.* Cashier *is seen behind the glass door, enters.* Lady *points to a chair, and starts to seat herself.* Cashier *stands.*]

Lady

I hope the bank— [Cashier *sees the picture, and starts violently.*] My visit to the bank was closely connected with this picture.

Cashier

[*Staring.*] You!

Lady

Do you find any point of resemblance.

CASHIER

[*Smiling*]: In the wrist!

LADY

Are you interested?

CASHIER

I should like to discover more.

LADY

Do such subjects interest you?

CASHIER

[*Looking straight at her*] Yes—I understand them.

LADY

Are there any more to be found here? You would do me a great favor—that's more important than the money.

CASHIER

I have the money.

LADY

I fear at this rate my letter of credit will soon be exhausted.

CASHIER

[*Produces a roll of bank notes*]: This will be enough.

LADY

I can only draw twelve thousand in all.

CASHIER

Sixty thousand!

LADY

But—how did you—?

CASHIER

That's my business.

LADY

How am I to—?

CASHIER

We shall bolt.

LADY

Bolt? Where?

CASHIER

Abroad. Anywhere. Pack your trunk, if you've got one. You can start from the station; I'll walk to the next stop and board the train. We'll spend the first night in—a time-table! [*He finds it.*]

LADY

Have you brought more than three thousand from the Bank?

CASHIER

[*Preoccupied with the time-table*]: I have sixty thousand in my pocket—50,000 in notes and ten thousand in gold.

LADY

And my part of that is—

CASHIER

[*Opens a roll of notes, and counts them with professional skill, then lays a bundle of them on the table*]: Your part. Take this. Put it away. We may be seen. The door has a glass panel. That's five hundred.

LADY

Five hundred?

CASHIER

More to come. All in good time. When we're in a safe place. Here we must be careful . . . hurry up—take it. No time for love-making. The wheel spins. An arm outstretched will be caught in the spokes. [*He springs to his feet.*]

LADY

But I need three thousand.

CASHIER

If the police find them on you, you'll find yourself in jail!

LADY

What have the police to do with it?

CASHIER

You were in the bank. Your presence filled the air. They'll suspect you; the link between us is clear as daylight.

LADY

I went to—your bank.

CASHIER

As cool as a cucumber—

LADY

I demanded—

CASHIER

You tried to.

LADY

I tried—

CASHIER

You did. With your forged letter.

LADY

[*Taking a paper from her handbag*]: Isn't my letter genuine?

CASHIER

As false as your diamonds.

LADY

I offered them as a security. Why should my precious stones be paste?

CASHIER

Ladies of your kind only dazzle.

LADY

What do you think I am? I'm dark, it's true; a Southerner, a Tuscan.

CASHIER

From Monte Carlo.

LADY

[*Smiles*]: No, from Florence!

CASHIER

[*His glance lighting upon the* SON'S *hat and cloak.*] Ha! Have I come too late?

LADY

Too late?

CASHIER

Where is he? I'll bargain with him. He'll be willing. I have the means. How much shall I offer? How high do you put the indemnity? How much shall I cram into his pockets? I'll bid up to fifteen thousand. Is he asleep? Still rolling in bed? Where's your room. Twenty thousand—five thousand extra for instant withdrawal! [*Picking up hat and cloak.*]

LADY

[*In astonishment*]: The gentleman is sitting in the lounge.

CASHIER

Downstairs? Too risky! Too many people down there. Call him up; I'll settle with him here. Ring for him; let the WAITER hustle. Twenty thousand, cash down! [*He begins counting the money.*]

LADY

Can my son speak for me?

CASHIER

[*Bounding back*]: Your—son!!!

LADY

I'm traveling with him. He's collecting material for a book on the history of art. That's what brought us from Florence to Germany.

CASHIER

[*Staring at her*]: Son?

LADY

Is that so appalling?

CASHIER

But—but—this picture—

LADY

A lucky find of his. My son is buying for three thousand marks; this was the amount needed so urgently. The owner is a wine dealer whom you will probably know by name. . . .

CASHIER

Furs . . . silk . . . rustle—glitter. The air was heavy with perfume!

LADY

This is mid-winter. As far as I know, my way of dressing is not exceptional.

CASHIER

The forged letter—

LADY

I was about to wire to my bank.

CASHIER

Your bare wrist—on which you wanted me to put the bracelet—

LADY

We're all clumsy with the left hand.

CASHIER

[*Duly, to himself*]: And I—have stolen the money—

LADY

[*Diverted*]: Will that satisfy you and your police? My son is not utterly unknown in the art world.

Cashier

Now—at this very moment—they've discovered everything! I asked for water to get the clerk out of the way—and again for water to get the porter away from the door. The notes are gone; I'm an embezzler. I mustn't be seen in the streets; I can't go to the railway station; the police are warned, sixty thousand! I must slip away across the fields—through the snow—before the whole town is on my track!

Lady

[*Shocked*]: Be quiet!

Cashier

I took all the money. Your presence filled the bank. Your scent hung on the air. You glistened and rustled—you put your naked hand in mine—your breath came warm across the counter—warm—

Lady

[*Silencing him*]: Please—I am a lady.

Cashier

But now you must—

LADY

[*Controlling herself*]: Tell me, are you married? Yes? [*Violent gesture from* CASHIER.] Ah, that makes a difference. Unless I am to consider the whole thing a joke, you gave way to a foolish impulse. Listen. You can make good the loss. You can go back to your bank and plead a passing illness—a lapse of memory. I suppose you still have the full amount.

CASHIER

I've embezzled the money—

LADY

[*Abruptly*]: Then I can take no further interest in the matter.

CASHIER

I've robbed the bank.

LADY

You grow tedious, my dear sir.

CASHIER

And now you must—

LADY

The one thing I must do, is to—

CASHIER

After this you must—

LADY

Preposterous.

CASHIER

I've robbed for you. I've delivered myself into your hands, destroyed my livelihood. I've burned my bridges behind me. I'm a thief and a criminal. [*Burying his face in his hands.*] Now you must! ... After all that you must!

LADY

[*Turns*]: I shall call my son. Perhaps he—

CASHIER

[*With a change of tone, springs nimbly to his feet. Grabbing her arm*]: Aha! Call him, would you? Rouse the hotel, give the alarm? A fine plan! Clumsy. I'm not so easily caught as that. Not in that trap. I have my wits about me, ladies and gentlemen. Yours are asleep. I'm always five miles ahead of you. Don't move. Stay where you are until I . . . [*He puts the money in his pocket.*] . . . until I . . . [*He presses his hat over his eyes.*] . . . until I . . . [*He wraps his coat closely about him.*] . . . until I . . . [*Softly he opens the glass door and slips out.* LADY *rises, stands motionless.*]

SON

[*Entering*]: The man from the bank has just gone out. You're looking worried, Mother. Is the money—?

LADY

I found this interview trying. You know, my dear boy, how money matters get on my nerves.

SON

Is there still trouble about the payment?

LADY

Perhaps I ought to tell you—

SON

Must I give back the picture?

LADY

I'm not thinking of that—

SON

But that's the chief question!

LADY

I think I ought to notify the police.

SON

Police?

LADY

Send this telegram to my bank. In future I must have proper documents that will satisfy every one.

SON

Isn't your letter of credit enough?

LADY

Not quite. Go to the telegraph office for me. I don't want to send the porter.

Son

And when shall we have the three thousand marks? [*Telephone bell rings.*]

Lady

[*Recoils*]: They're ringing me up already. [*At the instrument.*] Oh! Has arrived? And I'm to call for it myself? Gladly. [*Change of tone.*] I'm not in the least annoyed. Yes, of course. [*Change of tone.*] Florence is a long way off. And then the Italian postoffice—I beg your pardon? Oh, via Berlin—a round about way. That explains it. Not in the least. Thank you. In ten minutes. Good-by. [*To* Son.] All settled, my dear boy. Never mind the telegram. [*She tears up the form.*] You shall have the picture. Your wine dealer can come along. He'll get his money at the bank. Pack up your treasure. We go straight from the bank to the station. [*Telephoning while the* Son *wraps up the picture.*] The bill, please. Rooms 14 and 16. Yes, immediately. Please.

Curtain

SCENE III

SCENE: *Aslant a field deep in snow. Through a tangle of low-hanging branches, blue shadows are cast by the midday sun.*

CASHIER

[*Comes in backward, furtively*]: What a marvelous contraption a man is. The mechanism runs in his joints—silently. Suddenly faculties are stimulated, action results. My hands, for instance, when did they ever shovel snow? And now they dig through snow drifts without the slightest trouble. My footprints are all blotted out. I have achieved a complete incognito. [*Pause.*] Frost and damp breed chills. Before you know it you've got a fever and that weakens the will—a man loses control over his actions if he's in bed sick. He's easily tracked. [*Throws cuffs to ground.*] Lie there! You'll be missed in the wash! Lamentations fill the kitchen! A pair of cuffs is missing! A catastrophy in the tubs! Chaos! [*Pause.*] Strange! How keen my wits are! Here I work like mad to efface my tracks and then betray myself by two bits of dirty linen. It is always a trifle, an oversight—carelessness that betrays the criminal. [*Pause.*] I wonder what's going to happen. I am keyed up to the highest pitch! I have every reason to expect momentous discoveries. The last few hours prove it. This morning a trusted employee—fortunes passing through my hands. The Construction Company makes a huge deposit. At noon an out-and-out scoundrel. Up to all the tricks. The details of flight carefully worked out. Turn the trick and run. Marvelous accomplishment—and only half the day gone. I am prepared for anything. I know I can play the game. I am on the march! There is no turning back. I march—so out with your trumps without any fuss. I have put sixty thousand on a single card—it must be trumps. I play too high to lose. No nonsense—cards on the table—do you understand? Now you'll have to, my beautiful lady. Your cue—my silken lady, give it to me, my resplendent lady—or the scene will fall flat. [*Pause.*] Idiot—and you think you can act! Perform your natural duties—breed children and don't bother the prompter. Ah, I beg your pardon—you have a son—you are completely absolved. I withdraw my aspersions. Good-by, give my compliments to the manager of the bank. His very glances cover you with slime, but don't let that worry you. He's been robbed of sixty-thousand. His roof rattles and leaks—never mind, never mind—the Construction Co. will mend it for him. I release you from all obligations—you are dismissed—you can go! Stop! Permit me to thank you! What's that you say? Nothing to thank you for? Yes! There is. Not worth mentioning? You are joking. You are my sole creditor. How so? I owe you my life! Good God—I exaggerate? You have electrified me—set me free. One step toward you and I enter a land of miracles. And with this load in my breast pocket I pay cash for all favors. And now fade away. You are outbid. Your means are too limited. Remember you have a son. Nothing will be knocked down to you. I'm paying cash down. [*Pause.*] I have ready money. Come on—what's for sale? [*Pause.*] Snow? Sunlight—stillness—. Blue snow at such a price. Outrageous, profiteering. I decline the offer. Your proposition is not *bona fide*. [*Pause.*] But I must pay. I must spend, I've got the cash. Where are the goods that are worth the whole sum? Sixty thousand and the buyer to boot—flesh and bones—body and soul. Deal with me! Sell to me—I have the money, you have the goods—let us trade. [*The wind is blowing, the sun is overcast, disant thunder is heard.*] The earth is in labor—spring gales at last! That's better! I knew my cry could not be in vain. My demand was urgent. Chaos is insulted and will not be put to shame by my colossal deed of this morning. I knew it. In a case like mine never let up. Go at them hard—pull down their cloaks and you'll see something. [*The tree has changed to the form of a skeleton, the wind and thunder die down.*] Have you been sitting behind me all this time eavesdropping? Are you an agent of the police? Not in the ordinary narrow sense—but [*pause*] comprising all. Police of Fate? Are you the all-embracing answer to my emphatic question? Does your rather well ventilated appearance suggest the final truth—emptiness? That's somewhat scanty—very threadbare—in fact nothing! I reject the information as being too full of gaps. Your services are not required. You can shut your rag and bone shop. I am not taken in as easily as that. [*Pause.*] This procedure would be exceedingly simple—it's true—you would spare me further entanglements. But I prefer complications. So farewell—if that is possible, to you in your condition! I still have things to do. When one is traveling one can't enter every house on the road—not even at the friendliest invitations. I still have many obligations to fulfil before evening. You can't possibly be the first—perhaps the last—but even then only as a last resort. I won't want to do it. But, as I said, as a last resort—that's debatable. Ring me up at midnight —ask Central for my number. It will change from hour to hour. And excuse the coldness of my tone. We should be on friendlier terms, I know. We are closely bound. I really believe I carry you about with me now.

So, you see, we have come to a sort of understanding. That is a beginning which gives one confidence and backbone to face the future, whatever it is. I appreciate that fully. My most profound respects. [*After a peal of thunder and a last gust of wind the skeleton reverts to the tree. The sun comes out again.*] There—I knew it wouldn't last.

CURTAIN

SCENE IV

SCENE: *Parlor in* CASHIER'S *house. In the window-boxes, blown geraniums. Table and chairs. Piano right.* MOTHER [*hard of hearing*] *sits near the window.* FIRST DAUGHTER *is embroidering at the table.* SECOND DAUGHTER *is practising the overture to Tannhauser.* WIFE *comes and goes on the left. The clock ticks interminably.*

MOTHER

What's that you're playing?

FIRST DAUGHTER

The Overture to Tannhauser.

MOTHER

"O Tannenbaum" is another pretty piece.

WIFE

[*Entering*]: It's time I began to fry the chops.

FIRST DAUGHTER

Oh, not yet, Mama.

WIFE

No, it's not time yet to fry the chops.

MOTHER

What are you embroidering now?

FIRST DAUGHTER

Father's slippers.

WIFE

[*Coming to* MOTHER]: To-day we have chops for dinner.

MOTHER

Are you frying them now?

WIFE

Plenty of time. It's not twelve o'clock yet.

First Daughter

Not nearly twelve, Mama.

Wife

No, not nearly twelve.

Mother

When he comes, it will be twelve.

Wife

He hasn't come yet.

First Daughter

When Father comes, it will be twelve o'clock.

Wife

Yes. [*Exit.*]

Second Daughter

[*Stops playing, listens*]: Is that Father?

First Daughter

[*Listens*]: Father?

WIFE

[*Enters*]: Is that my husband?

MOTHER

Is that my son?

SECOND DAUGHTER

Father!

FIRST DAUGHTER

Father!

WIFE

Husband!

MOTHER

Son!

CASHIER

[*Enters right, hangs up hat and cloak. Pause.*]

WIFE

Where do you come from?

CASHIER

From the cemetery.

MOTHER

Has somebody died suddenly?

CASHIER

[*Patting her on the back*]: You can have a sudden death, but not a sudden burial.

WIFE

Where have you come from?

CASHIER

From the grave. I burrowed through the clods with my forehead. See, here's a lump of ice. It was a great effort to get through—an extraordinary effort. I've dirtied my hands a little. You need a good grip to pull yourself up. You're buried deep. Life keeps on dumping dirt on you. Mountains of it—dust—ashes—the place is a rubbish heap. The dead lie at the usual depth—three yards. The living keep on sinking deeper and deeper.

WIFE

You're frozen from head to foot.

CASHIER

Thawed. Shaken by storms, like the Spring. The wind whistled and roared; I tell you it stripped off my flesh until my bones were bare—a skeleton—bleached in a minute. A boneyard! At last the sun welded me together again. And here I am. Thus I've been renewed from the soles of my feet up.

MOTHER

Have you been out in the open?

CASHIER

In hideous dungeons, Mother. In bottomless pits beneath monstrous towers; deafened by clanking chains, blinded by darkness!

WIFE

The bank must be closed. You've been celebrating with the manager. Has there been a happy event in his family?

Cashier

He has his eye on a new mistress. Italian beauty —silks and furs—where oranges bloom. Wrists like polished ivory. Black tresses—olive complexion. Diamonds. Real . . . all real. Tus . . . tus . . . the rest sounds like Canaan. Fetch me an atlas. Tus-Canaan. Is that right? Is there an Island of that name? A mountain? A swamp? Geography can tell us everything. But he'll burn his fingers. She'll turn him down—brush him off like a bit of dirt. There he lies . . . sprawling on the carpet . . . legs in the air . . . our snug little manager!

Wife

The bank is not closed?

Cashier

Never, Wife. Prisons are never closed. The procession is endless. An eternal pilgrimage. Like sheep rushing into the slaughter house. A seething mass. No escape—none—unless you jump over their backs.

Mother

Your coat's torn in the back.

CASHIER

And look at my hat! Fit for a tramp.

SECOND DAUGHTER

The lining's torn.

CASHIER

Look in my pockets. Left . . . right! [FIRST DAUGHTER *and* SECOND DAUGHTER *pulls out cuffs.*]

CASHIER

Inventory.

DAUGHTERS

Your cuffs.

CASHIER

But not the buttons. Hat—coat—torn—what can you expect—jumping over backs. They kick—they scratch—hurdles and fences—silence in the pen—order in the fold—equal rights for all. But one jump—don't hesitate—and you are out of the pen. One mighty deed and here I am! Behind me nothing and before me—What? [*Sits. Pause.*]

WIFE

[*Stares at him.*]

MOTHER

[*Half-whispering*]: He's sick.

CASHIER

[*To one of the* DAUGHTERS]: Get my jacket. [*To the other*]: My slippers. [*To the first*]: My cap. [*To the other*]: My pipe. [*All are brought.*]

MOTHER

You oughn't to smoke, when you've already been—

WIFE

[*Motioning her to be silent*]: Shall I give you a light?

CASHIER

[*In jacket, slippers, and embroidered skull-cap, with pipe in hand, seats himself comfortably at the table.*] Light up!

Wife

[*Anxiously*]: Does it draw?

Cashier

[*Looking into pipe*]: I shall have to send it for a thorough cleaning. There must be some bits of stale tobacco in the stem. Sometimes way in . . . there are obstructions. It means I have to draw harder than is strictly necessary.

Wife

Do you want me to take it now?

Cashier

No, stay here. [*Blowing great smoke-clouds.*] It will do. [*To* Second Daughter]: Play something.

Second Daughter

[*At a sign from her mother, sits at piano and plays.*]

Cashier

What piece is that?

SECOND DAUGHTER

The Overture to Tannhauser.

CASHIER

[*Nods approval. To* FIRST DAUGHTER]: Sewing? Mending? Darning?

FIRST DAUGHTER

Embroidering your slippers.

CASHIER

Very practical. And you, Grandma?

MOTHER

[*Feeling the universal dread*]: I was just having forty winks.

CASHIER

In peace and quiet.

MOTHER

Yes, my life is quiet now.

CASHIER

[*To* WIFE]: And you, Wife?

WIFE

I was going to fry the chops.

CASHIER

[*Nodding*]: Mmm—kitchen.

WIFE

I'll fry yours now.

CASHIER

[*Nodding as before*]: Kitchen!

WIFE

[*Exit.*]

CASHIER

[*To* DAUGHTERS]: Open the doors.
[DAUGHTERS *exit right and left, returning immediately.*]

Wife

[*Enters. Pause*]: Are you too warm in here? [*She returns to her task.*]

Cashier

[*Looking around him*]: Grandmother at the window. Daughters—at the table embroidering . . . playing Wagner. Wife busy in the kitchen. Four walls . . . family life. Cozy . . . all of us together. Mother—son . . . child under one roof. The magic of familiar things. It spins a web. Room with a table. Piano. Kitchen . . . daily bread. Coffee in the morning . . . chops at noon. Bedroom . . . beds . . . in . . . out. More magic. In the end flat on your back . . . white and stiff. Table pushed against the wall . . . in the center a pine coffin . . . screw lid . . . silver mountings . . . but detachable . . . a bit of crepe on the lamp . . . piano unopened for a year.

Second Daughter

[*Stops playing, and runs sobbing into the kitchen.*]

Wife

[*Enters*]: She is practising the new piece.

MOTHER

Why doesn't she try something simpler?

CASHIER

[*Knocks out his pipe, begins putting on his hat and overcoat.*]

WIFE

Are you going to the bank? Are you going out on business?

CASHIER

Bank—business? No.

WIFE

Then where are you going?

CASHIER

That's the question, Wife. I've climbed down from wind-swept trees to find an answer. I came here first. Warm and cozy, this nest; I won't deny its good points; but it doesn't stand the final test. No! The answer is clear. This is not the end of my journey, just a sign-post; the road leads further on. [*He is now fully dressed.*]

Wife

[*Distraught*]: Husband, how wild you look!

Cashier

Like a tramp, as I told you. Never mind. Better a ragged wayfarer than an empty road!

Wife

But, it's dinner-time.

Mother

[*Half rising*]: And you're going out, just before a meal?

Cashier

I smell the pork chops. Full stomach, drowsy wits.

Mother

[*Beats the air suddenly with her arms, and falls senseless.*]

FIRST DAUGHTER

Grandma.

SECOND DAUGHTER

Grandma! Mother. [*Both fall on their knees, beside her.*

WIFE

[*Stands motionless.*]

CASHIER

[*Going to* MOTHER'*s chair*]: For once in his life a man goes out before his meal—and that kills her. [*He brushes the daughters aside and regards the body.*] Grief? Mourning? Overflowing tears? Can they make me forget. Are these bonds so closely woven that when they break there's nothing left to me in life but grief?—Mother—son! [*He pulls the roll of banknotes out of his pocket and weighs it in his hand, then shakes his head and puts the money away.*] Grief does not paralyze . . . the eyes are dry and the mind goes on. There's no time to lose, if my day is to be well spent. [*He lays his well-worn purse on the table.*] Use it. There's money honestly earned. That may be worth remembering. Use it. [*He goes out on the left.*]

WIFE

[*Stands motionless.*]

DAUGHTERS

[*Bend over the dead* MOTHER.]

BANK MANAGER

[*Coming from the right.*]: Is your husband at home? Has your husband been there? I have to bring you the painful news that he has absconded. We missed him some hours ago; since then we have been through his books. The sum involved is sixty thousand marks, deposited by the Realty Construction Co. So far, I've refrained from making the matter public, in the hope that he would come to his senses and return. This is my last attempt. You see I've made a personal call. Has your husband been here? [*He looks around him, and observes jacket, pipe, etc.*] It looks as though . . . [*His glance lights upon the group at the window. He nods.*] I see! In that case . . . [*He shrugs his shoulders, puts on his hat.*] I can only express my personal sympathy; be assured of that. The rest must take its course. [*Exit* MANAGER.]

Daughters

[*Coming to* Wife]: Mother—

Wife

[*Savagely*]: Don't screech into my ears! Who are you? What do you want? Brats—monkeys. What have you to do with me? [*Breaking down.*] My husband has left me.

Daughters

[*Stand shyly, holding hands.*]

Curtain

Setting by Lee Simonson *Photograph by Francis Bruguierre*
SCENE V. FROM THE THEATRE GUILD PRODUCTION

SCENE V

SCENE: The *steward's box of a velodrome during a cycle race meeting. Jewish gentlemen, stewards, come and go. They are all alike; little animated figures in dinner jackets, with silk hats tilted back and binoculars slung in leather cases. Whistling, catcalls and a restless hum from the crowded tiers of spectators unseen, off right. Music. All the action takes place on the platform.*

FIRST GENTLEMAN

[*Entering*]: Is everything ready?

SECOND GENTLEMAN

See for yourself.

FIRST GENTLEMAN

[*Looking through glasses*]: The palms—

SECOND GENTLEMAN

What's the matter with the palms?

FIRST GENTLEMAN

I thought as much.

SECOND GENTLEMAN

But what's wrong with them?

FIRST GENTLEMAN

Who arranged them like that?

THIRD GENTLEMAN

Crazy.

SECOND GENTLEMAN

Upon my soul, you're right!

FIRST GENTLEMAN

Was nobody responsible for arranging them?

THIRD GENTLEMAN

Ridiculous. Simply ridiculous.

FIRST GENTLEMAN

Whoever it was, he's as blind as a bat!

THIRD GENTLEMAN

Or fast asleep.

SECOND GENTLEMAN

Asleep. But this is only the fourth night of the races.

FIRST GENTLEMAN

The palm-tubs must be pushed on one side.

SECOND GENTLEMAN

Will you see to it?

FIRST GENTLEMAN

Right against the wall. There must be a clear view of the whole track. [*Exit.*]

THIRD GENTLEMAN

And of the royal box.

SECOND GENTLEMAN

I'll go with you. [*Exit.*]

FOURTH GENTLEMAN

[*Enters, fires a pistol-shot and withdraws.*]

FIFTH GENTLEMAN

[*Enters with a red lacquered megaphone.*]

THIRD GENTLEMAN

How much is the prize?

FIFTH GENTLEMAN

Eighty marks. Fifty to the winner, thirty to the second.

FIRST GENTLEMAN

[*Re-entering*]: Three times round, no more. We're tiring them out.

FOURTH GENTLEMAN

[*Through megaphone*]: A prize is offered of eighty marks. The winner to receive fifty marks, the second thirty marks. [*Applause.*]

SECOND AND THIRD GENTLEMEN

[*Return, one carrying a flag.*]

FIRST GENTLEMAN

We can start them now.

SECOND GENTLEMAN

Not yet. No. 7 is shifting.

FIRST GENTLEMAN

Off!

SECOND GENTLEMAN

[*Lowers his flag. The race begins. Rising and falling volume of applause, with silent intervals.*]

THIRD GENTLEMAN

The little fellows must win once in a while.

FOURTH GENTLEMAN

It's a good thing the favorites are holding back.

FIFTH GENTLEMAN

They'll have to work hard enough before the night's over.

Third Gentleman

The riders are terribly excited.

Fourth Gentleman

And no wonder.

Fifth Gentleman

Depend upon it, the championship will be settled to-night.

Third Gentleman

The Americans are still fresh.

Fifth Gentleman

Our lads will make them hustle.

Fourth Gentleman

Let's hope his royal highness will be pleased with the victory.

First Gentleman

[*Looking through glasses*]: The box is still empty. [*Outburst of applause.*]

Third Gentleman

The result!

Fourth Gentleman

Prizes in cash—50 marks for No. 11, 30 marks for No. 4.

[Seventh Gentleman *enters with* Cashier. *The latter is in evening clothes, with silk hat, patent shoes, gloves, cloak, his beard trimmed, his hair carefully brushed.*]

Cashier

Tell me what is this all about?

Second Gentleman

I'll introduce you to the stewards.

Cashier

My name doesn't matter.

Second Gentleman

But you ought to meet the management.

CASHIER

I prefer to remain incognito.

SECOND GENTLEMAN

But you seem interested in these races.

CASHIER

I haven't the slightest idea what it's all about. What are they doing down there? I can see a round track with a bright moving line, like a snake. Now one comes in, another falls out. Why is that?

SECOND GENTLEMAN

They ride in pairs. While one partner is pedalling—

CASHIER

The other blockhead sleeps?

SECOND GENTLEMAN

He's being massaged.

CASHIER

And you call that a relay race?

SECOND GENTLEMAN

Certainly.

CASHIER

You might as well call it a relay rest.

FIRST GENTLEMAN

[*Approaching*]: Ahem! The enclosure is reserved for the management.

SECOND GENTLEMAN

This gentleman offers a prize of a thousand marks.

FIRST GENTLEMAN

[*Change of tone*]: Allow me to introduce myself.

CASHIER

On no account.

SECOND GENTLEMAN

The gentleman wishes to preserve his incognito.

CASHIER

Impenetrably.

SECOND GENTLEMAN

I was just explaining the sport to him.

CASHIER

Yes, don't you find it funny?

FIRST GENTLEMAN

How do you mean?

CASHIER

Why, this relay rest.

FOURTH GENTLEMAN

A prize of a thousand marks! For how many laps?

CASHIER

As many as you please.

FROM MORN TO MIDNIGHT   85

FOURTH GENTLEMAN

How much shall we allot to the winner?

CASHIER

That's your affair.

FOURTH GENTLEMAN

Eight hundred and two hundred. [*Through megaphone.*] An anonymous gentleman offers the following prizes for an open race of ten laps: 800 marks to the winner; 200 marks to the second; 1000 marks in all. [*Loud applause.*]

SECOND GENTLEMAN

But tell me, if you're not really interested in this sort of thing, why do you offer such a big prize?

CASHIER

Because it works like magic.

SECOND GENTLEMAN

On the pace of the riders, you mean?

CASHIER

Rubbish.

THIRD GENTLEMAN

[*Entering*]: Are you the gentleman who is offering a thousand marks?

CASHIER

In gold.

SECOND GENTLEMAN

That would take too long to count. . . .

CASHIER

Watch me. [*He pulls out the money, moistens his finger and counts rapidly.*] That makes less to carry.

SECOND GENTLEMAN

I see you're an expert.

CASHIER

A mere detail, sir. [*Handing him the money.*] Accept payment.

SECOND GENTLEMAN

Received with thanks.

FIFTH GENTLEMAN

[*Approaching*]: Where is the gentleman? Allow me to introduce—

CASHIER

Certainly not!

THIRD GENTLEMAN

[*With flag*]: I shall give the start. [*General movement from the stand.*]

FIFTH GENTLEMAN

Now we shall see a tussle for the championship.

THIRD GENTLEMAN

[*Joining group*]: All the cracks are in the race.

FOURTH GENTLEMAN

Off! [*Outburst of applause.*]

CASHIER

[*Taking* FIRST *and* SECOND GENTLEMEN *by the collar and turning them around*]: Now I'll answer your question for you. Look up!

SECOND GENTLEMAN

But you must keep your eye on the track, and watch how the race goes.

CASHIER

Childish, this sport. One rider must win because the other loses. Look up, I say! It's there, among the crowd, that the magic works. Look at them— three tiers—one above the other—packed like sardines—excitement rages. Down there in the boxes the better classes are still controlling themselves. They're only looking on but, oh, what looks wide-eyed—staring. One row higher, their bodies sway and vibrate. You hear exclamations. Way up— no restraint! Fanatic—yells—bellowing nakedness —a gallery of passion. Just look at that group! Five times entwined; five heads dancing on one shoulder, five pairs of arms beating time across one howling breast! At the head of this monster is a single man. He's being crushed . . . mangled . . . thrust over the railing. His hat, crumpled, falls through the murky atmosphere . . . flutters into the middle balcony, lights upon a lady's bosom. There it rests daintily . . . so daintily! She'll never notice the hat; she'll go to bed with it; year in, year out, she'll carry this hat upon her breast!

[*The applause swells.*]

FIRST GENTLEMAN

The Dutchman is putting on speed.

CASHIER

The second balcony joins in. An alliance has been made; the hat has done the trick. The lady crushes it against the railing. Pretty lady, your bosom will show the marks of this! There's no help for it. It's foolish to struggle. You are pushed to the wall and you've got to give yourself, just as you are, without a murmur.

SECOND GENTLEMAN

Do you know the lady?

CASHIER

Look! Some one is being pushed out over the railing. He swings free, he loses his hold, he drops

—he sails down into the boxes. What has become of him? Vanished! Swallowed, stifled, absorbed! A raindrop in a maelstrom!

FIRST GENTLEMAN

The fellow from Hamburg is making up ground.

CASHIER

The boxes are frantic. The falling man has set up contact. Restraint can go to the devil! Dinner-jackets quiver. Shirt fronts begin to split. Studs fly in all directions. Lips are parted, jaws are rattling. Above and below—all distinctions are lost. One universal yell from every tier. Pandemonium. Climax.

SECOND GENTLEMAN

[*Turning*]: He wins! He wins! The German wins! What do you say to that?

CASHIER

Stuff and nonsense.

SECOND GENTLEMAN

A marvelous spurt!

CASHIER

Marvelous trash!

FIRST GENTLEMAN

[*About to leave*]: We'll just make certain—

CASHIER

[*Holding him back*]: Have you any doubts about it?

SECOND GENTLEMAN

The German was leading, but—

CASHIER

Never mind that, if you please. [*Pointing to the audience.*] Up there you have the staggering fact. Watch the supreme effort, the lazy dizzy height of accomplishment. From boxes to gallery one seething flux, dissolving the individual, recreating-passion! Differences melt away, veils are torn away; passion rules! The trumpets blare and the walls come tumbling down. No restraint, no modesty, no motherhood, no childhood—nothing but passion! There's the real thing. That's worth the search. That justifies the price!

Third Gentleman

[*Entering*]: The ambulance column is working splendidly.

Cashier

Is the man hurt who fell?

Third Gentleman

Crushed flat.

Cashier

When life is at fever heat some must die.

Fourth Gentleman

[*With megaphone*]: Result; 800 marks won by No. 2; 200 marks won by No. 1. [*Loud applause.*]

Fifth Gentleman

The men are tired out.

Second Gentleman

You could see the pace dropping.

Third Gentleman

They need a rest.

Cashier

I've another prize to offer.

First Gentleman

Presently, sir.

Cashier

No interruptions, no delays.

Second Gentleman

We must give them a chance to breathe.

Cashier

Bah! Don't talk to me of those fools! Look at the public, bursting with excitement. This power mustn't be wasted. We'll feed the flames; you shall see them leap into the sky. I offer fifty thousand marks.

Second Gentleman

Do you mean it?

THIRD GENTLEMAN

How much did you say?

CASHIER

Fifty thousand. Everything.

THIRD GENTLEMAN

It's an unheard of sum—

CASHIER

The effect will be unheard of. Warn your ambulance men on every floor.

FIRST GENTLEMAN

We accept your offer. The contest shall begin when the box is occupied.

SECOND GENTLEMAN

Capital idea!

THIRD GENTLEMAN

Excellent!

Fourth Gentleman

This is a profitable visitor.

Fifth Gentleman

[*Digging him in the rib*]: A paying guest.

Cashier

[*To* First Gentleman]: What do you mean—when the box is occupied?

First Gentleman

We'll talk over the conditions in the committee room. I suggest 30,000 to the winner; 15,000 to the second; 5,000 to the third.

Second Gentleman

Exactly.

Third Gentleman

[*Gloomily*]: Downright waste, I call it.

Fifth Gentleman

The sport's ruined for good and all.

First Gentleman

[*Turning*]: As soon as the box is occupied. [*All go out, leaving* Cashier *alone. Enter* Salvation Lass.]

Salvation Lass

The War Cry! Ten pfennigs, sir.

Cashier

Presently, presently.

Salvation Lass

The War Cry, sir.

Cashier

What trash are you trying to sell?

Salvation Lass

The War Cry, sir.

Cashier

You're too late. The battle's in full swing.

SALVATION LASS

[*Shaking tin box*]: Ten pfennigs, sir.

CASHIER

So you expect to start a war for ten pfennigs?

SALVATION LASS

Ten pfennigs, sir.

CASHIER

I'm paying an indemnity of 50,000 marks.

SALVATION LASS

Ten pfennigs.

CASHIER

Yours is a wretched scuffle. I only subscribe to pitched battles.

SALVATION LASS

Ten pfennigs.

CASHIER

I carry only gold.

SALVATION LASS

Ten pfennigs.

CASHIER

Gold—

SALVATION LASS

Ten—

CASHIER

[*Seizing megaphone, bellows at her through it*]: Gold! Gold! Gold! [SALVATION LASS *goes out. Many* GENTLEMEN *enter.*]

FOURTH GENTLEMAN

Would you care to announce your offer yourself?

CASHIER

No, I'm a spectator. You stun them with the 50,000. [*Handing him the megaphone.*]

Setting by Lee Simonson   SCENE VI. FROM THE THEATRE GUILD PRODUCTION   Photograph by Francis Bruguiere

FOURTH GENTLEMAN

[*Through the megaphone*]: A new prize is offered by the same anonymous gentleman. [*Cries of "Bravo!"*] The total sum is 50,000 marks. 5,000 marks to the third, 15,000 to the second. The winner to receive 30,000 marks. [*Ecstasy.*]

CASHIER

[*Stands apart, nodding his head*]: There we have it, the pinnacle. The summit. The climbing hope fulfilled. The roar of a spring gale. The breaking wave of a human tide. All bonds are burst. Up with the veils—down with the shams! Humanity—free humanity, high and low, untroubled by class, unfettered by manners. Unclean, but free. That's a reward for my impudence. [*Pulling out a bundle of notes.*] I can pay with a good heart! *Sudden silence. The* GENTLEMEN *have taken off their silk hats and stand with bowed heads.*]

FOURTH GENTLEMAN

[*Coming to* CASHIER]: If you'll hand me the money, we can have the race for your prize immediately.

CASHIER

What's the meaning of this?

FOURTH GENTLEMAN

Of what, my dear sir?

CASHIER

Oh this sudden, unnatural silence.

FOURTH GENTLEMAN

Unnatural? Not at all. His Royal Highness has just entered his box.

CASHIER

Highness . . . the royal box . . . the house full.

FOURTH GENTLEMAN

Your generous patronage comes at the most opportune moment.

CASHIER

Thank you! I don't intend to waste my money.

FOURTH GENTLEMAN

What do you mean?

CASHIER

I find the sum too large . . . as a subscription to the Society of back benders!

FOURTH GENTLEMAN

But pray explain . . .

CASHIER

This fire that was raging a moment ago has been put out by the boot of his Highness. You take me for crazy, if you think I will throw one single penny under the snouts of these grovelling dogs, these crooked lackeys! A kick where the bend is greatest, that's the prize they'll get from me.

FOURTH GENTLEMAN

But the prize has been announced. His Royal Highness is in his box. The audience is showing a proper respect. What do you mean?

CASHIER

If you don't understand my words, let deeds speak for me. [*With violent blow he crushes the other's silk hat down upon his shoulders. Exit.* FOURTH GENTLEMAN *rushes after him, but is restrained by the others.*]

CURTAIN

SCENE VI

SCENE: *Private supper room in a cabaret. Subdued dance music.*

WAITER

[*Opens the door.*]

CASHIER

[*Enters; evening clothes, coat, silk muffler, gold-headed bamboo cane.*]

WAITER

Will this room suit you, sir?

CASHIER

It'll do.

WAITER

[*Takes coat, etc.*]

CASHIER

[*Turns his back and looks into a mirror.*]

WAITER

How many places shall I lay, sir?

CASHIER

Twenty-four. I'm expecting my grandma, my mother, my wife, and several aunts. The supper is to celebrate my daughter's confirmation.

WAITER

[*Stares at him.*]

CASHIER

[*To the other's reflection in the mirror*]: Ass! Two! What are these private rooms for?

WAITER

What brand would you prefer?

CASHIER

Leave that to me, my oily friend. I shall know which flower to pluck in the ball-room . . . round or slender, a bud or a full-blown rose. I shall not require your invaluable services. No doubt they are invaluable . . . or have you a fixed tariff for that too?

WAITER

What brand of champagne, if you please?

CASHIER

Ahem! Grand Marnier.

WAITER

That's the liqueur, sir.

CASHIER

Then I leave it to you.

WAITER

Two bottles of Pommery—extra dry. [*Producing menu card.*] And for supper?

CASHIER

Pinnacles!

Waiter

Oeufs pochés Bergère? Poulet grillé? Steak de veau truffé? Parfait de foi gras en croûte? Salade coeur de laitue?

Cashier

Pinnacles, pinnacles from soup to dessert.

Waiter

Pardon?

Cashier

[*Tapping him on the nose*]: A pinnacle is the point of perfection . . . the summit of a work of art. So it must be with your pots and pans. The last word in delicacy. The menu of menus. Fit to garnish great events. It's your affair, my friend. I'm not the cook.

Waiter

[*Sets a large menu-card on the table*]: It will be served in twenty minutes. [*He rearranges glasses, etc. Heads with silken masks peep through the doorway.*]

CASHIER

[*Sees them in the mirror. Shaking a warning finger at them*]: Wait, my moths! Presently I shall have you in the lamplight! [*The masks vanish, giggling.*]

WAITER

[*Hangs a notice—"Reserved"—on the outside of the door, then withdraws and closes it behind him.*]

CASHIER

[*Pushes back his silk hat, takes out a gold cigarette case, strikes a match, sings*]: "Tor . . . ea . . . dor, Tor . . . ea . . . dor . . ." Queer, how this stuff comes to your lips. A man's mind must be cram full of it . . . cram full. Everything. Toreador—Carmen—Caruso. I read all this somewhere . . . it stuck in my head. There it lies, piled up like a snowdrift. At this very moment I could give a history of the Bagdad railway. And how the Crown Prince of Roumania married the Czar's second daughter, Tatjana. Well, well, let them marry. The people need princes. [*Sings.*] "Tat . . . tat . . . ja . . . na, Tat . . . ja . . . na . . ." [*Twirling his cane, exit.*]

WAITER

[*Enters with bottles on ice. Uncorks, pours out wine. Exit.*]

CASHIER

[*Re-enters, driving before him a female* MASK *in a harlequin's red and yellow-quartered costume.*] Fly, moth! Fly, moth!

FIRST MASK

[*Running round the table*]: Fizz! [*She drinks both of the filled glasses.*] Fizz!

CASHIER

[*Pouring out more wine*]: Liquid powder. Load your painted body.

FIRST MASK

[*Drinking*]: Fizz!

CASHIER

Battery mounted, action front.

FIRST MASK

Fizz!

CASHIER

[*Putting aside the bottles*]: Loaded. [*Coming to her.*] Ready to fire.

FIRST MASK

[*Leans drunkenly towards him.*]

CASHIER

[*Shaking her limp arm*]: Look brighter, moth.

FIRST MASK

[*Does not respond.*]

CASHIER

You're dizzy, my bright butterfly. You've been licking the prickly yellow honey. Open your wings, enfold me, cover me up. I'm an outlaw; give me a hiding-place; open your wings.

FIRST MASK

[*With a hiccough*]: Fizz!

CASHIER

No, my bird of paradise. You have your full load.

FIRST MASK

Fizz! [*Sinking onto sofa.*]

CASHIER

Not another drop, or you'll be tipsy. Then what would you be worth?

FIRST MASK

Fizz!

CASHIER

How much are you worth? What have you to offer? [*Bending over her.*]

FIRST MASK

Fizz!

CASHIER

I gave you that, but what can you give me?

FIRST MASK

[*Falls asleep.*]

CASHIER

Ha! You'd sleep here, would you? Little imp! But I've no time for the joke; I find it too tedious. [*He rises, fills a glass of wine and throws it in her face.*] Good morning to you! The cocks are crowing!

FIRST MASK

[*Leaping to her feet*]: Swine!

CASHIER

A quaint name. Unfortunately I'm traveling incognito, and can't respond to the introduction. And so, my mask of the well-known snoutish family . . . get off my sofa!

FIRST MASK

I'll make you pay for this!

CASHIER

I've paid already. It was cheap at the price.

FIRST MASK

[*Exit.*]

CASHIER

[*Drinks champagne. Exits, singing.*]

WAITER

[*Enters with caviare; collects empty glasses. Exit.*]

CASHIER

[*Enters with two black* MASKS.]

SECOND MASK

[*Slamming the door*]: Reserved!

THIRD MASK

[*At the table*]: Caviare!

SECOND MASK

[*Running to her*]: Caviare?

CASHIER

Black as your masks. Black as yourselves. Eat it up; gobble it, cram it down your throats. [*Seating himself between them.*] Speak caviare. Sing wine. I've no use for your brains. [*He pours out champagne and fills their plates.*] Not one word shall you utter. Not a syllable, not an exclamation. You shall be dumb as the fish that strewed this black spawn upon the Black Sea. You can giggle, you can bleat, but don't talk to me. You've nothing to say. You've nothing to shed but your finery ... Be careful! I've settled one already!

MASKS

[*Look at one another, sniggering.*]

CASHIER

[*Taking* SECOND MASK *by the arm*]: What color are your eyes? Green ... yellow? [*Turning to* THIRD MASK.] And yours? Blue ... red? A play of glances through the eyeholes. That promises well. Come, I'll offer a beauty prize!

MASKS

[*Laugh.*]

CASHIER

[*To* SECOND MASK]: You're the pretty one. You struggle hard, but wait! In a moment I'll tear down your curtain and look at the show.

SECOND MASK

[*Breaks away from him.*]

CASHIER

[*To* THIRD MASK]: You have something to hide. Modesty's your lure. You dropped in here by chance You were looking for adventure. Well, here's your adventurer. Off with your mask.

THIRD MASK

[*Slips away from him.*]

CASHIER

This is the goal? I sit here trembling. You've stirred my blood. Now let me pay. [*He pulls out a bundle of notes and divides it between them.*] Pretty mask, this for your beauty. Pretty mask, this for your beauty. [*Holding his hand before his eyes.*] One—two—three!

MASKS

[*Lift their dominoes.*]

CASHIER

[*Looking at them, laughs hoarsely*]: Cover them—cover them up! [*He runs round the table.*] Monsters—horrors! Out with you this minute—this very second,—or I'll . . . [*He lifts his cane.*]

SECOND MASK

But you told us—

THIRD MASK

You wanted us—

CASHIER

I wanted to get at you!

MASKS

[*Run out.*]

CASHIER

[*Shaking himself, drinks champagne*]: Sluts! [*Exits, humming.*]

WAITER

[*Enters with fresh bottles, and exit.*]

CASHIER

[*Kicking the door open, entering with* FOURTH MASK, *a Pierrette in a domino cloak reaching to her shoes. He leaves her standing in the middle of the room, and throws himself in chair*]: Dance!

FOURTH MASK

[*Stands still.*]

CASHIER

Dance! Spin your bag of bones. Dance, dance! Brains are nothing. Beauty doesn't count. Dancing's the thing—twisting, whirling! Dance, dance, dance!

FOURTH MASK

[*Comes halting to the mirror.*]

CASHIER

[*Waving her away*]: No interruption, no delay. Dance!

FOURTH MASK

[*Stands motionless.*]

CASHIER

Why don't you leap in the air? Have you never heard of Dervishes? Dancing-men. Men while they dance, corpses when they cease. Death and dancing—sign posts on the road of life. And between them—

SALVATION LASS

[*Enters.*]

CASHIER

Oh, Halleluja!

SALVATION LASS

The War Cry!

CASHIER

I know. Ten pfennigs.

SALVATION LASS

[*Holds out her box.*]

CASHIER

When do you expect me to jump into your box?

SALVATION LASS

The War Cry!

CASHIER

I suppose you do expect it?

SALVATION LASS

Ten pfennigs.

CASHIER

When will it be?

SALVATION LASS

Ten pfennigs.

CASHIER

So you mean to hang on to my coat-tails, do you?

SALVATION LASS

[*Shakes her box.*]

CASHIER

I'll shake you off!

SALVATION LASS

[*Shakes box.*]

CASHIER

[*To* MASK]: Dance!

SALVATION LASS

Oh! [*Exit.*]

FOURTH MASK

[*Comes to table.*]

CASHIER

Why were you sitting in a corner of the ballroom, instead of dancing in the middle of the floor? That made me look at you. All the others went whirling by, and you were motionless. Why do you wear a long cloak, when they are dressed like slender boys?

FOURTH MASK

I don't dance.

CASHIER

You don't dance like the others.

FOURTH MASK

I can't dance.

CASHIER

Not to music, perhaps; not keeping time. You're right; that's too slow. But you can do other dances. You hide something under your cloak—your own particular spring, not to be cramped by step and measure! You have a quicker movement—a nimbler leap. [*Pushing everything off the table.*] Here's your stage. Jump on to it. A boundless riot in this narrow circle. Jump now. One bound from the carpet. One effortless leap—on the springs that are rooted in your joints. Jump. Put spurs to your heels. Arch your knees. Let your dress float free over the dancing limbs!

FOURTH MASK

[*Sits on the edge of the table*]: I can't dance.

CASHIER

You arouse my curiosity. Do you know what price I can pay? [*Showing her a roll of bank notes.*] All that!

FOURTH MASK

[*Takes his hand and passes it down her leg*]: You see—I can't.

CASHIER

[*Leaping to his feet*]: A wooden leg! [*He seizes a champagne cooler and upsets it over her.*] I'll water it for you! We'll make the buds sprout!

FOURTH MASK

I'll teach you a lesson.

CASHIER

I'm out to learn!

Fourth Mask

Just wait! [*Exit.*]

Cashier

[*Puts a bank note on the table, takes cloak and stick. Exit.*]
[Guests *in evening dress enter.*]

First Guest

Where is the fellow?

Second Guest

Let's have a closer look at him.

First Guest

A blackguard who entices away our girls—

Second Guest

Stuffs them with caviare—

Third Guest

Drenches them in champagne—

SECOND GUEST

And then insults them!

FIRST GUEST

We'll find out his price—

SECOND GUEST

Where is he?

THIRD GUEST

Given us the slip!

FIRST GUEST

He smelt trouble!

SECOND GUEST

The place was too hot for him.

THIRD GUEST

[*Finding the bank note*]: A thousand!

SECOND GUEST

Good God!

FIRST GUEST

He must stink of money.

SECOND GUEST

That's to pay the bill.

THIRD GUEST

He's bolted. We'll do a vanishing trick too. [*He pockets the money.*]

FIRST GUEST

That's the indemnity for our girls.

SECOND GUEST

Now let's give them the slip.

THIRD GUEST

They're all drunk.

FIRST GUEST

They'll only dirty our shirt-fronts for us.

SECOND GUEST

Let's go to the district for a week.

THIRD GUEST

Bravo! While the money lasts! Look out, here comes the waiter!

WAITER

[*Entering with full tray, halts dismayed.*]

FIRST GUEST

Are you looking for any one?

SECOND GUEST

You might find him under the table. [*Laughter.*]

WAITER

[*In an outburst*]: The champagne—the supper—the private room—nothing paid for. Five bottles of Pommery, two portions of caviare, two special suppers—I have to stand for everything. I've a wife and children. I've been four months out of a place, on account of a weak chest. You won't see me ruined, gentlemen?

Third Guest

What has your chest to do with us? We all have wives and children.

Second Guest

Did we do you? What are you talking about?

First Guest

What sort of a place is this? Where are we? It's a common den of swindlers. And you lure people into a place like this? We're respectable people who pay for their drinks. Eh! What! Eh!

Third Guest

[*After changing the door-key to the outer side*]: Look under the table, there. Now we've paid you, too! [*He gives the* Waiter, *who turns round, a push which sends him sprawling.*]

Waiter

[*Staggers, falls.*]

Gentlemen

[*Exeunt.*]

WAITER

[*Rises, runs to the door, finds it locked. Beating his fists on the panels*]: Let me out! Let me out! You needn't pay me! I'm going—into the river!

CURTAIN

Setting by Lee Simonson SCENE VII. FROM THE THEATRE GUILD PRODUCTION Photograph by Francis Bruguiere

SCENE VII

SCENE: *Salvation Army hall, seen in depth. The background is formed by a black curtain. In front of this stands the low platform on which is the penitent form.*

In the body of the hall, the benches are crowded. A great hanging lamp, with a tangle of wires for electric lighting, is above the audience. In the foreground on the left, is the entrance. Music: "Jesus Lover of my Soul," played on an organ, and sung by the audience. From a corner, applause and laughter centering in one man.

SOLDIER

[SALVATION LASS *goes to this corner and sits near the disturber. She takes his hand in hers and whispers to him.*]

VOICE

[*From the other side*]: Move up closer. Be careful, Bill! Ha, ha! Move there!

Soldier

[Salvation Lass, *goes to the speaker, a young workman.*]

Workman

What are you after?

Soldier

[*Looks at him, shaking her head gravely*]: Merriment.

Officer

[*Woman of* 30, *coming to the front of the platform*]: I've a question to ask you all.

Some

[*Cry*]: Hush! [*Or whistle for silence.*]

Others

Speech. None of your jaw! . . . Music! . . .

Voices

Begin! Stop!

OFFICER

Tell me . . . why are you sitting crowded there?

VOICE

Why not?

OFFICER

You're packed like herrings in a barrel. You're fighting for places . . . shoving one another off the forms. Yet one bench stands empty.

VOICE

Nothing doing!

OFFICER

Why do you sit squeezing and crowding there? Can't you see it's a nasty habit? Who knows his next-door neighbor? You rub shoulders with him, you press your knees against his, and for all you know he may be rotting. You look into his face—and perhaps his mind is full of murderous thoughts. I know there are sick men and criminals in this hall. So I give you warning! Mind your next-door neighbor! Beware of him! Those benches groan under sick men and criminals!

Woman's Voice

Next to me?

Second Voice

Or me?

Officer

I give you this word of advice; steer clear of your neighbor! In this asphalt city, disease and crime are everywhere. Which of you is without a scab? Your skin may be smooth and white, but your looks give you away. You have no eyes to see, but your eyes are wide open to betray you. You haven't escaped the great plague; the germs are too powerful. You've been sitting too long near bad neighbors. Come up here, come away from those benches, if you would not be as your neighbors are in this city of asphalt. This is the last warning. Repent. Repent. Come up here, come to the penitent form. Come to the penitent form, come to the penitent form. [*Music, "Jesus Lover of My Soul."*]

Salvation Lass

[*Leads in* Cashier.]

Cashier

[*In evening dress, arouses some notice.*]

SALVATION LASS

[*Finds* CASHIER *a place among the crowd, stands next to him and explains the procedure.*]

CASHIER

[*Looks around him amused. Music ceases, ironical applause.*]

OFFICER

[*Coming forward again*]: One of our comrades will tell you how he found his way to the penitent bench.

FIRST SOLDIER

[*Young man steps onto the platform.*]

VOICE

So that's the mug! [*Some laughter.*]

FIRST SOLDIER

I want to tell you of my sin. I led a life without giving a thought to my soul. I cared only for my body. I built up my body like a strong wall; the soul was quite hidden behind it. I sought for glory with my body, and made broader the shadow in which my soul withered away. My sin was sport. I practised it without a moment's pause; vain of the quickness of my feet on the pedals; and the ring of the applause among the spectators. I sent out many a challenge; I won many a prize. My name was printed on every bill board; my picture was in all the papers. I was in the running for the world championship. . . . At last my soul spoke to me. Its patience was ended. I met with an accident. The injury was not fatal. My soul wanted to leave me time for repentence. My soul left me strength enough to rise from those benches where you sit, and to climb up here to the penitent form. There my soul could speak to me in peace. What it told me I can't tell you now. It's all too wonderful, and my words are too weak to describe it. You must come yourselves, and hear the voice speak within you! [*He steps in.*]

A Man

[*Laughs obscenely.*]

Several

[*Cry*]: Hush!

SALVATION LASS

[*To* CASHIER, *in a low voice*]: Do you hear him?

CASHIER

Let me alone. [*Music plays and ceases.*]

OFFICER

[*Coming forward*]: You've heard our comrade's testimony. Can you win anything nobler than your own? And it's quite easy, for the soul is there within you. You've only to give it peace . . . once, just once. The soul wants to sit with you for one quiet hour. Its favorite seat is on this bench. There must be one among you who sinned like our comrade here. Our comrade will help him. The way has been opened up. So come. Come to the penitent bench. Come to the penitent bench. Come to the penitent bench. [*Silence.*]

FIRST PENITENT

[*Young man of powerful build, with one arm in a sling, rises in a corner of the hall and makes his way through the crowd, smiling nervously. He mounts the platform.*]

MAN

[*Laughs obscencly.*]

ANOTHER

[*Indignantly*]: Where is that dirty lout!

MAN

[*Rises abashed, and makes his way toward the door.*]

OTHERS

That's the fellow!

SOLDIER

[SALVATION LASS, *hurries to him and leads him back to the place.*]

VOICE

[*Facetiously*]: Oh, let me go, Angelina!

SEVERAL OTHERS

Bravo!

First Penitent

[*On the platform*]: In this city of asphalt there's a hall. Inside the hall is a cycle-track. This was my sin. I was a rider too. I was a rider in the relay races this week. On the second night I met with a collision. I was thrown; my arm was broken. The races are hurrying on, but I am at rest. All my life I have been riding without a thought. Now! I want to think of everything. [*Loudly.*] I want to think of my sins at the penitent bench. [*Led by a* Soldier, *he sinks on to the bench;* Soldier *remains at his side.*]

Officer

A soul has been won! [*Music plays and ceases.*]

Salvation Lass

[*To* Cashier]: Do you see him?

Cashier

My affair. My affair.

Salvation Lass

What are you muttering?

CASHIER

The relay races.

SALVATION LASS

Are you ready?

CASHIER

Hold your tongue.

OFFICER

[*Stepping forward*]: Another comrade will testify.

MAN

[*Hisses.*]

OTHERS

Be quiet there!

SECOND SOLDIER

[*Girl mounts the platform*]: Whose sin is my sin? I'll tell you of my sin without shame. I had a

wretched home, if you could call it a home. The
man, a drunkard, was not my father. The woman—
who was my mother—went with smart gentlemen.
She gave me all the money I wanted; her bully gave
me all the blows—I didn't want. [*Laughter.*] No
one thought of me; least of all did I think of myself.
So I became a lost woman. I was blind in those
days. I couldn't see that the miserable life at home
was only meant to make me think of my soul and
dedicate myself to its salvation. One night I learned
the truth. I had a gentleman with me, and he
asked me to darken the room. I turned out the gas,
though I wasn't used to such ways. Presently I
understood why he had asked me; for, I realized that
I had with me only the trunk of a man whose legs
had been cut off. He didn't want me to know that he
had wooden legs, and that he had taken them off in the
dark. Then horror took hold of me, and wouldn't
let me go. I began to hate my body; it was only my
soul that I could love. And now this soul of mine
is my delight. It's so perfect, so beautiful; it's the
bonniest thing I know. I know too much of it to
tell you here. If you ask your souls, they'll tell you
all—all! [*She steps down. Silence.*]

OFFICER

[*Coming forward*]: You've heard our sister testify. Her soul offered itself to her, and she did

not refuse. Now she tells you her story with joyful lips. Isn't a soul offering itself now, at this moment, to one of you? Let it come closer. Let it speak; here on this bench it will be undisturbed. Come to the penitent bench. Come to the penitent bench. [*Movement in the hall. Some turn round.*]

Second Penitent

[*Elderly prostitute, begins to speak as she comes forward*]: What do you think of me, ladies and gentlemen? I was just tired to death of street walking, and dropped in by chance for a rest. I'm not shy—oh, dear no! I don't know this hall; it's my first time here. Just dropped in by chance, as you might say. [*Speaking from the platform.*] But you make a great mistake, ladies and gentlemen, if you think I should wait to be asked a second time! Not this child, thank you—oh, dear no! Take a good look at me, from tip to toe; it's your last chance; enjoy the treat while you can! It's quite all right; never mind me; I'm not a bit shy; look me up and down. Thank you, my soul's not for disposal. I've never sold that. You could offer me as much as you pleased, but my soul was always my own. I'm obliged to you for your compliments, ladies and gentlemen. You won't run up against me in the streets again. I've got no time to spare for you. My soul leaves me no peace. ['A SOLDIER *leads her to the penitent form.*]

OFFICER

A soul has been won! [*Music. Jubilation of the* SOLDIERS. *Music ceases.*]

SALVATION LASS

[*To* CASHIER.] Do you hear all?

CASHIER

That's my affair. My affair.

SALVATION LASS

What are you muttering about?

CASHIER

The wooden leg. The wooden leg.

SALVATION LASS

Are you ready?

CASHIER

Not yet. Not yet.

A MAN

[*Standing upright in the middle of the hall*]: Tell me my sin. I want to hear my sin!

OFFICER

[*Coming forward*]: Our comrade here will tell you.

VOICES

[*Excitedly*]: Sit down! Keep quiet; give him a chance.

THIRD SOLDIER

[*Elderly man*]: Let me tell you my story. It's an everyday story.

VOICE

Then why tell it?

Third Soldier

That's how it came to be my sin. I had a snug home, a contented family, a comfortable job. Everything was just—everyday. In the evening, when I sat smoking my pipe at the table, under the lamp, with my wife and children round about me, I felt satisfied enough. I never felt the need of a change. Yet the change came, I forget what started it; perhaps I never knew. The soul knocks quietly at your door. It knows the right hour and uses it.

Second Penitent

Halleluja.

Third Soldier

However that might be, I couldn't pass the warning by. I stood out at first in a sluggish sort of way, but the soul was stronger. More and more I felt its power. All my born days I'd been set upon comfort now I knew that nothing could satisfy me fully but the soul.

Soldiers

Halleluja.

Third Soldier

I don't look for comfort any longer at the table under the lamp, with a pipe in my mouth; I find it here alone at the penitent bench. That's my everyday story. [*He stands back.*]
[*Music plays and is interrupted by* Third Penitent. *Elbowing his way up*]: My sin! My sin! [*From the platform.*] I'm the father of a family!

Voice

Congratulations!

Third Penitent

I have two daughters. I have a wife. My mother is still with us. We live in four rooms. It's quite snug and cozy in our house. One of my daughters plays the piano, the other does embroideries. My wife cooks. My old mother waters the geraniums in the window-boxes. It's cozy in our house. Coziness itself. It's fine in our house. It's grand . . . first-rate . . . It's a model—a pattern of a home. [*With a change of voice.*] Our house is loathsome . . . horrible . . . horrible . . . mean . . . paltry through and through. It stinks of paltriness in every room; with the piano-playing, the cooking, the embroidery, the watering pots. [*Breaking out.*]

I have a soul! I have a soul! I have a soul! [*He stumbles to the penitent bench.*]

SOLDIERS

Halleluja.

OFFICER

A soul has been won!

SALVATION LASS

[*To* CASHIER]: Do you see him?

CASHIER

My daughters. My wife. My mother.

SALVATION LASS

What do you keep mumbling?

CASHIER

My affair. My affair.

SALVATION LASS

Are you ready?

CASHIER

Not yet. Not yet.
[*Jubilant music. Loud uproar in the hall.*]

MAN

[*Standing upright, and stretching out hands*]: What's my sin? What's my sin? I want to know my sin? Tell me my sin.

OFFICER

[*Coming forward*]: Our comrade will tell you. [*Deep silence.*]

FOURTH SOLDIER

[*Middle-aged, comes forward*]: My soul had a hard struggle to win the victory. It had to take me by the throat and shake me like a rat. It was rougher still with me. It sent me to jail. I'd stolen the money that was entrusted to me; I'd absconded with a big sum. They caught me; I was tried and sentenced. In my prison cell I found the rest my soul had been looking for. At the last it could speak to me in peace. At last I could hear its voice. Those days in the lonely cell became the happiest in my life. When my time was finished I could not part from my soul.

Soldiers

Halleluja.

Fourth Soldier

I looked for a quiet place where we two could meet. I found it here on the penitent form: I find it here still, each evening that I feel the need of a happy hour! [*Standing aside.*]

Officer

[*Coming forward*]: Our comrade has told you of his happy hours at the penitent form. Who is there among you who wants to escape from this sin? Here he will find peace! Come to the penitent bench!

Man

[*Standing up, shouting and gesticulating*]: Nobody's sin! That's nobody's sin! I want to hear mine! My sin! My sin! [*Many join in.*] My sin! My sin! My sin!

CASHIER

My sin!

SALVATION LASS

[*Above the uproar*]: What are you shouting?

CASHIER

The bank. The money.

SALVATION LASS

[*Shaking him*]: Are you ready?

CASHIER

Yes, now I'm ready!

SALVATION LASS

[*Taking his arm*]: I'll lead you up there. I'll stand by you—always at your side. [*Turning to the crowd, ecstatically*]: A soul is going to speak. I looked for this soul. I found this soul! [*The tumult ebbs into a quiet hum.*]

CASHIER

[*On the platform*, SALVATION LASS *by his side*]: I've been on the road since this morning. I was

driven out on this search. There was no chance
of turning back. The earth gave way behind me,
all bridges were broken. I had to march forward
on a road that led me here. I won't weary you with
the halting-places that wearied me. None of them
were worth my break with the old life; none of
them repaid me. I marched on with a searching eye,
a sure touch, a clear head. I passed them all by,
stage after stage; they dwindled and vanished in the
distance. It wasn't this, it wasn't that, or the next
—or the fourth or the fifth! What is the goal, what
is the prize, that's worth the whole stake? This hall,
humming with crowded benches, ringing with melody!
This hall! Here, from bench to bench, the spirit
thunders fulfilment! Here glow the twin crucibles;
confession and repentance! Molten and free from
dross, the soul stands like a glittering tower, strong
and bright. You cry fulfilment for these benches.
[*Pause.*] I'll tell you my story.

Salvation Lass

Speak, I'm with you. I'll stand by you.

Cashier

I've been all day on the road. I confess; I'm
a bank cashier. I embezzled the money that was entrusted me. A good round sum; sixty thousand
marks! I fled with it into your city of asphalt.

By this time, they're on my track; perhaps they've offered a big reward. I'm not in hiding any more. I confess! You can buy nothing worth having, even with all the money of all the banks in the world. You get less than you pay, every time. The more you spend, the less the goods are worth. The money corrupts them: the money veils the truth. Money's the meanest of the paltry swindles in this world! [*Pulling rolls of bank notes out of his breast pocket.*] This hall is a burning oven; it glows with your contempt for all mean things. I throw the money to you; it shall be torn and stamped under foot. So much less deceit in the world! So much trash consumed. I'll go through your benches and give myself up to the first policeman; after confession, comes atonement. So the cup is filled!

[*With gloved hands he scatters bank notes broadcast into the hall. The money flutters down; all hands are stretched upward; a scrimmage ensues. The crowd is tangled into a fighting skein. The* SOLDIERS *leap from the platform; benches are overturned, blows of fisticuffs resound above the shouting. At last, the cramped mass rolls to the door and out into the street.*]

SALVATION LASS

[*Who has taken no part in the struggle, stands alone on the steps.*]

CASHIER

[*Smiling at her*] : You are standing by me. You are with me still! [*Picking up an abandoned drum and a stick.*] On we go. [*Roll of drum.*] The crowd is left behind. [*Roll of drum.*] The yelping pack outrun. Vast emptiness. Elbow room! Room! Room! Room! [*Drum.*] A maid remains . . . upright, steadfast! Maiden and man. The old garden is reopened. The sky is clear. A voice cries from the silent tree tops. It is well. [*Drum.*] Maiden and man . . . eternal constancy. Maiden and man . . . fulness in the void. Maiden and man . . . the beginning and the end. Maiden and man . . . the seed and the flower. Maiden and man . . . sense and aim and goal! [*Rapid drumtaps, then a long roll.*]

SALVATION LASS

[*Draws back to the door, and slips out.*]

CASHIER

[*Beats a tattoo.*]

SALVATION LASS

[*Throws the door open. To* POLICEMAN]: There he is! I've shown him to you! I've earned the reward.

Cashier

[*Letting fall the drumstick in the middle of a beat*]: Here above you, I stand. Two are too many. Space holds but one. Space is loneliness. Loneliness is space. Coldness is sunshine. Sunshine is coldness. Fever heat burns you. Fever heat freezes you. Fields are deserted. Ice overgrows them. Who can escape? Where is the door?

Policeman

Is this the only entrance?

Salvation Lass

[*Nods.*]

Cashier

[*Feels in his pocket.*]

Policeman

He's got a hand in his pocket. Switch off that light. We're a target for him!

Salvation Lass

[*Obeys. All the lights of the hanging lamp are put out. Lights from the left illuminate the tangle of wires, forming a skeleton in outline.*]

CASHIER

[*Feeling with his left hand in his breast pocket, grasps with his right a trumpet, and blows a fanfare toward the lamp*]: Ah!— Discovered. Scorned in the snow this morning—welcomed now in the tangled wires. I salute you. [*Trumpet.*] The road is behind me. Panting, I climb the steep curves that lead upward. My forces are spent. I've spared myself nothing. I've made the path hard, where it might have been easy. This morning in the snow when we met, you and I, you should have been more pressing in your invitation. One spark of enlightenment would have helped me and spared me all trouble. It doesn't take much of a brain to see that—Why did I hesitate? Why take the road? Whither am I bound? From first to last you sit there, naked bone. From morn to midnight, I rage in a circle ... and now your beckoning finger points the way ... whither? [*He shoots the answer into his breast.*

POLICEMAN

Switch on the light.

SALVATION LASS

[*Does so.*]

CASHIER

[*Has fallen back, with arms outstretched, tumbling headlong down the steps. His husky gasp is like an "Ecce," his heavy sigh is like a "Homo." One second later all the lamps explode with a loud report.*]

POLICEMAN

There must be a short circuit in the main. [*Darkness.*]

CURTAIN

THE END

Milton Keynes UK
Ingram Content Group UK Ltd.
UKHW040853050124
435493UK00005B/763